Growing
Garden Flowers
Indoors

Growing
Garden Flowers
Indoors

⋞❀⋟

By JACK KRAMER

Drawings by Michael G. Valdez

A Sunrise Book
E. P. Dutton & Co., Inc.
New York

Published simultaneously in Canada by
Clarke, Irwin & Company Limited, Toronto and Vancouver
ISBN: 0-87690-197-6 (cloth)
0-87690-223-9 (paper)

Library of Congress Cataloging in Publication Data
Kramer, Jack, 1927–
    Growing garden flowers indoors.
    Bibliography: p.
    Includes index.
    1. Window-gardening.   2. Flower gardening.
3. Container gardening. I. Title.
SB419.K717 1976   635.9′65   75-25749

[CONTENTS]

Growing
Garden Flowers
Indoors

ᵔᵓ ❀ ᵓᵔ

Flowers to You

If you have always envied people with gardens, now you too can have colorful flowers—without a backyard or extensive grounds! You can grow outdoor flowers indoors in pots and tubs as room decoration or to cut for arrangements. Brilliant nasturtiums in pots can grace your kitchen window, and rows of lovely petunias and bellflowers (campanulas) can brighten a dining room. Tulips and all kinds of bulbous lilies in ornamental containers will announce spring long before it arrives outdoors, and such plants as browallias will be colorful late into autumn, even though gray days may be on the way. All this beauty is yours when you grow outdoor plants indoors in pots.

Whether you live in an apartment or a house, there are always places for lovely blooms, and raising garden flowers inside is no more difficult than growing house plants. Not all garden flowers will adapt to pot culture, but many will—enough to keep your home or apartment decked in bloom from spring through winter.

You can grow your own plants from seed or buy prestarted plants from nurseries in season. In addition to the standard annuals and perennials (and a few shrubs) try flowering bulbs and vines. And here's a pleasant surprise: most of these plants are inexpensive, compared with "house" plants.

So give your house plants some company and start growing nasturtiums and other flowering plants at your windows. In no time you will be a gardener indoors even though you have no garden outdoors. Mother nature is generous with her bounty, and in this book I hope to tell you how to capture some of her beauty for your very own.

Jack Kramer

❧ ❀ ❧

Your Flower Garden Indoors

Often we envy country dwellers or people with outdoor gardens because of their beautiful flowers. But some of this beauty is also available for indoor gardeners from the many varieties of annuals and perennials, shrubs, bulbs, and flowering vines. Only certain plants will take to indoor situations, but there are enough of them to turn any window in any apartment or home into a colorful flower garden.

I have grown nasturtiums on my window sills for several years, and these bright flowers bloom as long or longer indoors as in the yard. My nasturtiums were a product of chance. I started the seeds in pots, and when they germinated and started to grow, I simply forgot to plant them outdoors and they remained at the window. Flushed with my first success, I tried other outdoor flowers indoors. When blue campanulas bloomed in late fall and impatiens almost throughout winter, I realized I had an outdoor garden indoors—and so can you.

Annuals and perennials comprise the majority of our garden flowers. Annuals live and bloom in one season, while perennials bloom, die, and come back the following year. Although you cannot carry over perennials in pots (unless you sink the pots in

Petunias and primroses in pots bring color indoors and add a note of cheer. (Photo by Guy Burgess.)

the garden soil), even for one season of color they are worth the money. After all, a dozen roses cost fifteen dollars and last only a week. Garden flowers can be used in pots at the windows or on a table to decorate the home. The basic premise of all this indoor bounty is not a miracle. It is simply a matter of knowing what to grow, how to start it, and what to grow it in to create a parade of flowers even in the bleakest months of the year.

A barrage of tulips and hyacinths, so colorful against the window in this winter scene. (Photo by Carl Moorestown.)

Where to Put Plants

Even the smallest apartment has some room for potted flowers; it is only a matter of finding that bare niche or nook and making it a colorful garden. You need very little space to grow a few petunias or nasturtiums. Indeed, these plants do just fine in six-inch pots, which fit a window sill or a shelf at a window.

The one requirement for placing plants is that there be some sun; flowers do need sun, so south or east light is best. Even in a west window you will get some harvest, although hardly an abundance of bloom. If north light is all that is available, then grow something else, such as foliage plants; annuals and perennials simply will not bear flowers in north light.

In case you have some good natural light, but a pot or container will not fit the area, then building your own wooden containers to suit the space really makes sense. Anyone can wield a hammer and nail a few pieces of wood together to make some handsome planters for flowers (see Chapter 3).

The Best Outdoor Flowers for Indoors

As I have already mentioned, you cannot have a lovely English garden of lupine and stock in your kitchen window. But you can grow many flowers. I think my favorites are nasturtiums and petunias. These colorful flowering plants do amazingly well indoors and continue to bloom for many months. Starting your own plants from seed costs little and is so simple that even a child can do it successfully. We outline these methods in Chapter 5.

So nasturtiums and petunias—and there are many varieties—lead the way as indoor garden performers. But potted marigolds, zinnias, and chrysanthemums do very well, too. And do not forget bulbs, such as crocuses, veltheimias, agapanthuses—all literally hidden treasures. The flowers are already in the bulb, and all you do is get them started. Many vines are also luxuriant indoor growers, and if you have space, bougainvillaea and morning glories can turn your window into a kaleidoscope of eye-pleasing color.

No longer envy your neighbor with that outdoor garden. Believe me, with annuals, perennials, bulbs, vines, and shrubs too, you can create a jungle that may take over the window and the room in short time, even if you do not work hard. These outdoor flowering plants have an amazing will to live and seem to enjoy being indoors as much as you enjoy having them there with you.

For Use as Cut Flowers

Vines and bulbs will decorate a specific area, but annuals and perennials can decorate any room in the home as cut flowers. Petunias, chrysanthemums, and nasturtiums all last amazingly long after they are cut. To use nasturtiums effectively indoors, put these dramatic flowers in a low vase by themselves. Do not add greenery or fern fronds or anything; just a simple bouquet will be lovely. Petunias, however, because they branch somewhat need a larger container and green leaves to make them really show up strongly. "Mums," of course, do well by themselves in a tall vase.

You can use a lot of cut flowers in a vase—brimful—or only a few for stark beauty, but anything in between is uninteresting. In other words, use a mass of flowers or very few.

To keep cut flowers as long as possible, replenish water daily; some flowers can drink up more water than you might think. Every other day recut stems at an angle to help them soak up water. The woody stems of some flowers should be slightly smashed before they are put into water.

For Pot Decoration

Pots of flowers generally used at windows can be moved to any area in the home for a few days as decoration but should

Pretty zinnias in pots furnish seasonal color; lovely additions at the windows. (Photo Burpee Seed Co.)

then be returned to a bright place. Colorful blooms are desirable additions on tables or desks and are a pleasant relief from the ubiquitous green plant. For example, group several small pots of primroses for a lovely display; use some tall lilies in a pot on a pedestal if you want vertical accent.

Flowering bulbs are easy to grow, so use masses of them to spotlight an area. Narcissus are always delightful, but try some of the lesser-known bulbs, such as the handsome, long-lasting zephyranthes, in pots or as cut flowers. The midget varieties of agapanthus, such as 'Peter Pan,' are delightful accompaniments to any room and grow well even away from windows. Many others can be used to make your indoor areas as colorful as outdoors. And best of all, there is no great expense involved, no great care necessary, to grow most of these fine plants.

❧ ❀ ☙

Tender Loving Care

Growing flowering plants indoors offers a new and exciting challenge to people who have grown only standard house plants such as philodendrons and dracaenas. Unfortunately, we have erroneously believed that outdoor flowers are only for outdoors. But the improved varieties of plants and improved home conditions (better humidity and ventilation) now enable us to have many outdoor plants as permanent indoor residents. Nasturtiums and impatiens *can and do* flourish at windows, as do dozens of other garden flowers.

Not *all* plants will adapt to indoor culture, but a great many will. If your first attempts are not successful and you lose a few plants, do not fret. You can always try again because garden plants are inexpensive, compared with regular house plants. But to make these outdoor treasures thrive indoors, you must have certain preliminary information about growing plants. (More detailed cultural instructions are given in later chapters under individual plants.)

> In this handsome garden room, the plants are beautifully grown and in the peak of health: chrysanthemums and azaleas are resplendent with color. (Photo by Max Eckert.)

The basic requirements of garden flowers (annuals and perennials) are plenty of moisture, good sunlight, and some feeding. Most outdoor plants will adapt readily to indoor temperatures of 78F by day and 65F at night. Indeed, a great many plants do require cool nights to prosper, and this is ideal for indoor gardening because there is less heat at night in most apartments and homes.

Seeds of some plants can be started directly in soil, but many plants do better in a seed mix until they are ready to be transplanted to pots when they are a few inches high. It is best to start many seeds (they are inexpensive) and then thin out the weak plants, keeping only the strong ones.

Annuals have to be replaced yearly. Perennials last for several years outdoors, but usually last only a season indoors. Some vines (many are evergreen) can be grown year-round, and most bulbous plants will be with you for many years.

Light

Light is a determining factor for a good harvest of flowers. Indoors, plants need all the sun they can get, and this generally means a southern, eastern, or western exposure. If you have only north windows, it is better to grow just foliage plants—flowering ones simply will not have many blooms.

It is important to remember that light coming through panes of glass is not as strong as natural light. To get more light to your plants, there are two things you can do: (1) paint the top and side jambs white to reflect more light, or apply aluminum foil to these areas to achieve the same effect; (2) use artificial light (this is explored later in the chapter). Plant lamps that fit ordinary light sockets provide the needed supplemental light so that special apparatus is not necessary.

Watering, Feeding

The plants we discuss in this book require more water than ordinary house plants. Remember that outdoor plants are fast-growing and thus always need moisture at the roots. This does not mean you should keep the soil sopping wet; just be sure it is always evenly moist.

When you water, do it thoroughly. Allow excess water to pour from drainage holes so the entire root system is moist. If the bottom is dry, air pockets form and roots die off because water cannot reach them.

Once a week try to let pots soak in a sink with water up to the soil level for about fifteen minutes or until air bubbles break on the surface of the soil. Once a month leach the plants by running water through the soil several times to eliminate any toxic salts that may have built up from too much feeding.

Packaged foods for plants are sold under various trade names, and they all contain nitrogen for good foliage growth, phosphorous to promote healthy stems and roots, potassium to keep the plant healthy, and other trace elements. The elements are always listed by percentage and in the same order: nitrogen, phosphorous, and potassium. A good, all-purpose, mild fertilizer would be one labeled 10-10-5, meaning 10% nitrogen; 10% phosphorous; 5% potassium.

For your flowering plants you want a 10-10-5 plant food because it is neither too weak nor too strong. Apply it with every second watering *only* when plants are putting out new growth. In addition, once a month add bone meal (one teaspoon dissolved in one quart of water) to promote blooming. You should need no other food supplements for your flowers.

New or ailing plants do not need feeding. New ones in fresh soil have enough nutrients, and ailing ones simply cannot absorb additional food. Once seedlings are growing, wait a few weeks and then start a biweekly feeding program.

Humidity

Humidity was formerly a nemesis for most plant-growers. But today many homes and apartments are equipped with heating and ventilating systems that provide good air circulation, and humidity adequate for people, as well as plants (about 30 to 40 percent). If you have many plants growing together, they will create their own humidity; plants transpire through their leaves. To keep moisture in the air, spray the growing area with tepid water from a misting bottle every day or so; it will help you and your plants, too.

Soil

Most people do not want to bother with special soil mixes for their plants. Rather, they use a good all-purpose packaged house-plant soil, and this is fine. Some are good, but do not pick just any soil at a nursery. You want a rich, porous soil, soft and flaky to the touch, one that contains all the necessary nutrients.

Follow these few suggestions when buying soil:

Give the package a good squeeze, as you would a loaf of bread. This will at least tell you whether the soil is porous and crumbly, which is what you want. If there is not too much printed material on the sack, you can sometimes determine a good soil by color: rich, friable soil is a dark blackish brown. Another fair test of good soil is by smell: rich soils smell earthy. However, this last test is hardly practical because you would have to open the package, something most nurseries would frown on. If you buy the bulk soil that most nurseries use for plants (and this is preferable), then of course you can run your hand through it and smell it, too.

An average package of soil is generally enough for four or five six-inch pots. To this standard house plant mix, add one cup of humus (also available in packages) and two tablespoons of bone meal. This will provide sufficient nutrients to get plants to bloom.

For plants requiring special types of soil, the following table lists the necessary additives for a six-inch pot:

TYPE OF SOIL	ADDITIVE	AMOUNT
acid	peat moss	one Tbsp.
coarse	{ sand { pebbles	{ five Tbsp. { five Tbsp.
fibrous	pebbles	five Tbsp.
rich	humus	five Tbsp.
sandy	sand	five Tbsp.

See Chapter 9 for information on keeping plants free of insects and diseases.

Potting and Repotting

The first potting of a plant is usually done with seedlings or prestarted plants. You transplant the young plants from the seed trays to pots of fresh soil at the start of the growing season, usually in spring. Repotting refers to removing an old plant from a container and putting it in fresh soil, as you would do annually for bulbous plants.

Potting a plant is simple. First, be sure the pot is clean. Insert small pieces of broken pots over the drainage hole; add a thin layer of gravel, and one teaspoon of charcoal chips (for a six-inch pot). Put in a mound of soil and center the plant on it. If the plant is too high, take out some soil; if it is too low, add some soil. Now fill in around the plant with fresh soil, and pack it around the collar of the plant. Tamp the pot down on a wooden surface to settle the soil. The plant should not be too deeply embedded in the soil or stand too far above the soil line. Now push down the soil firmly, but not too tightly, with your thumbs. Leave ½ inch between the soil line and the top of the pot to allow for watering.

Artificial Light

Artificial light used as supplemental light for plants allows us to have plants in shady areas. Hobbyists who grow their plants in special carts or tray set-ups generally use fluorescent lamps, but for our purposes the new incandescent lamps made especially for plant growth are ideal. They can be placed in standard light sockets, are readily available, and require no special equipment (reflectors and so forth).

The plant-grow lights are sold under various trade names, and your electrical supply store can furnish information about them. Be sure to place the lamp at least thirty inches from the top of the plants so excessive heat does not harm foliage. One 150-watt lamp (flood type) is all that is needed for a small window garden; leave it on twelve to fourteen hours a day. For starting seeds, a combination of fluorescent and incandescent light is generally used; two 40-watt fluorescent lamps with a reflector work well along with two or three 8-watt incandescent lamps.

For more information on artificial light growing consult the many good books on the subject at your library.

CHAPTER 3

ᦥ ❀ ᦥ

Containers,
Planters, and Whatnot

A chapter on containers may seem superfluous, but what you put a plant into is important if you want a totally beautiful window garden. There are many new plant containers: the conventional pots and tubs or more elaborate housings, such as clay planters (rectangular and square), lovely cachepots, glazed pots, and so forth.

Standard terra-cotta pots are still popular and are now available in many new designs. You may want to build (or have built) wooden boxes for specific areas. (See pp. 26–28.)

No matter what you grow your plants in, try to arrange a balanced, pleasing picture rather than a hodgepodge of pots at a window. There are so many new containers at various prices that it is wise to shop around before making your selection.

Terra-Cotta Pots

These pots are excellent for the window sill. Generally, a four- or five-inch pot is the largest that can be accommodated at a window even if you have shelves, and this will, of course, restrict your choice of plants. Use pots of one design to create a uniform look—the results will be very attractive. The best terra-cotta container is an azalea pot, which is squat and low, because it looks good at windows. To protect sills from moisture, use saucers with cork mats in them, or elevate pots in saucers on thin strips of redwood (½ inch by ½ inch) spaced ¼ inch apart. This allows air to circulate under the pots at the same time.

I generally use terra-cotta pots because their porous walls allow moisture to escape slowly, which is beneficial to plants. And because the pots come in so many sizes and designs, there is always a wide choice to select from. However, if the natural color does not harmonize with your room decor, use the clay pot that is painted on the outside. Although these pots discourage moisture evaporation, they are still satisfactory and very handsome.

Always be sure all pots are scrupulously clean. Clay pots can become slimy and encrusted with dirt, so occasionally scrub them to keep them handsome. Always soak new clay pots overnight in water or they will absorb the water the plants need.

Wooden Containers

Custom detailing always creates a striking total window scene, and your own wooden containers let you work with the space available and thus utilize every inch. Wood is the easiest and most popular material because it is inexpensive and it harmonizes well with most interiors.

Redwood and cedar are the best woods for planters; they resist moisture and do not tend to rot. They need no outside finish and will weather beautifully over the years. However, if you want some decorative effect, you can score, groove, or even sandblast them for a unique designed effect. Wood can also be painted to match existing color schemes.

Douglas fir, a very strong wood, and pine, a soft wood, can also be used if you apply suitable preservatives. However, some preservatives contain noxious chemicals that can harm plants.

Redwood boxes are ideal containers for flowering plants such as tulips and primroses. Note the different sizes of the boxes and how handsome they are. (Photo courtesy California Redwood Association.)

Try Penta (trade name for pentochlorophyl), which is satisfactory and harmless. Inside the container a galvanized metal liner can be used instead of preservatives, but this is expensive and has to be specially made at a sheet-metal shop. An alternative is a plastic tray. Plastic trays of all types are sold at nurseries and kitchen shops.

You can nail boxes together, but glue and screws will ensure a better and stronger box. One-inch lumber is fine for most small boxes, such as eight by sixteen or twenty inches. Most boxes for flowers should be at least four to six inches deep, with mitered corners. The bottom of a box may be redwood slats spaced ¼ inch apart (to allow excess water to drain) or exterior plywood with holes drilled for drainage.

A simple rectangular box, four inches deep and made from one-inch redwood, is ideal for small flowering plants like campanulas or felicias. I use brass screws to fasten the sides, ¾-inch lumber for the bottom, and I drill two or three ¼-inch drainage holes at the bottom.

A cube planter is neat and functional. For a twelve-inch box, use one- by twelve-inch finished redwood. Stain, paint, or use the redwood as it is. Nail or screw the corners together and attach the bottom board.

All wooden boxes and planters for window sills or shelves will need some type of metal or plastic trays under them to catch excess water. Suppliers sell these two- or three-inch shallow trays. Pastel colors are preferable to garnish colors that may clash with plants.

Cachepots

These handsome decorative pots add glamour to any window. You can plant directly in them or merely use them to hold potted plants. If you plant directly, use newer cachepots because they have drainage holes.

Cachepots come in many sizes and shapes: hexagons, rectangles, and circles. Some pots have exterior floral decoration, and others feature geometric designs, but most have a flair of elegance that is often lacking in other containers. A footed cachepot elevates the plant somewhat and makes it a more complete piece.

Planters

The old is becoming the new in all things today, including plant containers. There is currently a renaissance of the Roman-type, clay plant boxes. These handsome planters are narrow or square in shape, with exterior motifs. Although primarily for outdoors, they are exceptionally handsome indoors, too. Widths and depths vary considerably, but in all cases these boxes are unique housings for plants.

Because of their weight and size (generally too wide for window sills), you may have to modify windows somewhat to use these planters. Attach a board to the existing window sill, and brace it underneath with a wooden block or legs, if necessary. You can plant directly in the boxes or simply use them as ornamental cover-ups to hold potted plants. Search for these fine containers because they are well worth your effort.

Plastic and Glazed Pots

Flexible plastic pots come in many colors but generally are not acceptable for plants if you want good looks. Furthermore, they deteriorate rapidly. The rigid plastic pots, also available in colors, are somewhat more attractive and do last for some time. For best results, use all one color at a window, rather than a conglomeration of colors, which tends to create a spotty effect. Acrylic pots cost more money than other flexible or rigid plastic pots, but they are worth the extra expense because their clear, glass-like elegance enhances beautiful flowers such as nasturtiums and

These handsome urns and planters are excellent housings for plants; they are simple in design and yet totally attractive. (Photo by Matthew Barr.)

petunias. Remember that water will not evaporate quickly from the soil because plastic is a nonporous material. This can be good or bad, depending on how neglectful you are about watering your plants. You will need to learn the proper amounts of water to give your plants in plastic containers, so be careful the first few weeks and water sparingly.

Glazed containers are very decorative and come in many lovely colors, some shiny in appearance, others with a matte finish. (I like the handsome, painted terra-cotta pots that have a shiny surface.) Years ago glazed pots never had drainage holes, but today most do. And it is imperative that you get pots with drainage holes for your plants—completely watertight containers require very careful watering or the soil will become waterlogged. This is especially harmful to flowering plants, which require very good water drainage.

Cover-ups

Cover-ups are enclosures for pots. They are made of various materials, such as wicker and rattan. One popular cover-up is the striking wicker basket with a metal ring inside. Use a clay saucer in the bottom of the basket to catch dripping water, and merely insert the pot so that the rim fits into the ring. Before you buy, make sure a basket has the iron ring insert that holds the pot.

For a quick and inexpensive new look, flexible bamboo or wicker wraparound cover-ups are quite satisfactory and lend the decorative note wanted.

Shelving

To really have a bounty of flowers at your windows, you will need shelves to accommodate pots. Glass and acrylic are the most popular shelving materials because they allow light to enter and are easy to work with. You can buy glass cut to size at glass dealers and attach a wooden block to each side of the window frame to hold the shelves. Use ³⁄₁₆-inch-thick glass. Be sure the edges of the glass are finished and smooth. Make shelves at least six inches wide (eight inches is even better), so pots do not slip off if accidentally brushed by your hand or arm.

Although pre-fabricated shelf kits (with glass and hardware) are available, I have yet to see any that I think are substantial, so be wary if you use them. Inspect them carefully to be sure they will fit your windows and will hold the weight of several potted plants.

Wood shelving is also used at windows, and I must admit to a partiality for wood. Redwood looks good and has a nice warm

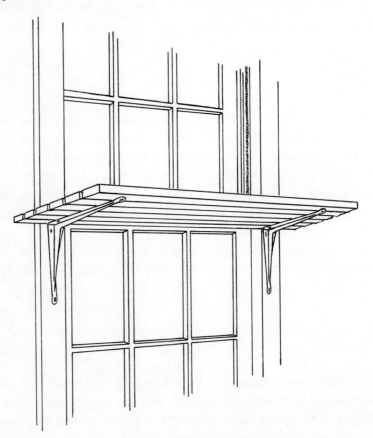

feeling to it. To install redwood shelves, you will need metal L-shaped brackets (available at hardware stores in six- to twelve-inch lengths with predrilled holes at both ends). Nail or screw one bracket to each side of the window at the required height and attach slats of one-inch redwood spaced ¼ inch apart on top of the brackets so that they stretch across the window. Use six slats for a seven inch shelf.

The main problem with shelves at windows is opening the windows after the shelves are installed. But you will not have any difficulty if you attach the brackets to the outer frames and leave a two-inch clearance between the shelves and the windows. However, if you have windows without framing or space for brackets, simply use pot rings at the sides of the windows and add some hanging plants suspended from ceiling hardware.

NOTE: Window shelves should not span more than thirty-six inches in width.

Vases for Cut Flowers

Because you will be using many of your plants for cut flowers, do get two or three glass vases. They come in all sizes and shapes, and may be inexpensive or costly. Ideally, you should have a small, a medium, and a large vase for your flower arrangements. I am especially fond of glass vases because stems and leaves are almost as attractive as flowers. But, of course, an opaque container will suffice.

Many glass vases come with flared lips, which make arranging flowers a snap. All you have to do is cut the flowers, grasp them in your hand, and set them into the vase; naturally, they will form a lovely halo of color, and the stems will crisscross in the water to form interesting patterns. (See Chapter 4 for flower-arranging tips.)

ঙ১ ✿ ৡ৶

Getting the Gold
from Your Flowers

If you are growing flowers indoors, there are definite plusses. Cut flowers in a vase and flowering plants in decorative pots and ornamental containers add highly dramatic and eye-pleasing accents to any decor. Flowers are an effective and inexpensive way to decorate your place, making your home bright and colorful even when the weather is cold and gray. For example, a row of cyclamens will brighten a dining table, and a group of potted "mums" can be the focal point at a stairwell. In this chapter I will discuss some of the exciting ways to use flowers as an integral part of your home decorating plan. Your rooms will suddenly become vibrant and inviting—all from the stunning impact of indoor flowers.

Cut Flowers

Once buds have formed, flowers can be cut for indoor beauty; put them in a vase of water and place the vase anywhere in a room. You may want to take a course in flower arranging given by a local garden club, or you may want to read some of the excellent books available on the subject. But briefly, here are the six basic rules of flower arranging:

1. Use either a *lot* of flowers or *very few* for a handsome effect.
2. Mix and match colors so they harmonize with one another and with the room.
3. Arrange flowers in various overall shapes: circles, crescents, curves, right angles, and triangles.
4. Keep the flower arrangement in proper proportion to the size of the vase.
5. Use dark flowers in a low arrangement, bright hues in a tall one.
6. Mix shapes of flowers; consider contrasting shapes, such as rounded blooms and pointed leaves.

When flowers are fully open, use small shears to make a diagonal cut, retaining as much stem as possible. (The diagonal cut exposes more of the cells to water than a straight cut does.) For woody-stemmed plants you will need to use a sharp knife.

Simple arrangements are quite effective and use fewer flowers; you can always buy flowers from a florist to supplement your own supply. However, remember that florist flowers will not be as fresh as your own. Indeed, they may be three days old before you get them!

To refresh or revive flowers cut off the bottom two inches of stem and plunge the flowers under water in a bucket—tepid water is best. Every other day give them fresh water to stand in. When flowers are almost spent, you can use them in still another way: cut the stems at the bases of the blossoms, and float the florets in water in shallow bowls.

Most cut flowers will last in a cool room for one week or longer, however, heat and drafts desiccate the blooms. Some people add copper pennies, salt, or aspirin to the water to make flowers last longer, but I do not think these additives make much difference. The best flowers for cutting are asters, azaleas, bach-

Containers for flowers should be simple; this metal urn is perfect for a small bouquet of flowers. (Photo by Matthew Barr.)

elor's buttons, calendulas, carnations, daffodils, chysanthemums (many kinds), hollyhocks, larkspur, marigolds, narcissus, nasturtiums, sweet peas, tulips, and zinnias.

Potted Flowers As Room Decoration

Hanging Gardens

Petunias and nasturtiums in hanging containers are splendidly handsome; they create accents wherever you use them and fill otherwise useless space over windows. And generally, plants in hanging containers grow better than plants at windows because they get better ventilation and light.

Today there are many containers with attached hardware especially designed for plants that trail. The best one I have seen is a wicker basket with a metal insert (mentioned in Chapter 3), which holds both pot and saucer, thus preventing water from spilling onto the floor. Some clay pots also come with a saucer attachment for cascading beauties.

Remember that hanging planters filled with soil are heavy, so strong supports are necessary. Hardware stores carry eyebolts, screw eyes, brackets, and other ceiling hardware that will hold the chains or ropes for supporting containers.

Arrange the baskets in tandem—that is, link the holder of one pot into the bottom drainage hole of the other pot. Be careful when doing this. After you hang the first basket from the ceiling or a wall bracket, turn the second basket sideways and insert its U-shaped hook into the drainage hole of the main basket. Then carefully turn the second basket upright. You want to avoid breaking the pot or damaging the plant. You have just created a column of color!

To plant a hanging basket, use standard packaged soil or bulk soil. Put some pot shards over the drainage hole of the container, fill in with two to three inches of soil, and set plants on the mound. If the plants seem too low, add some soil; if they are

Hanging pottery such as these containers are beautiful in themselves and filled with pretty flowers are outstanding. (Photo by author.)

too high, remove some soil. Now fill in and around the mound with more soil, using a potting stick (a wooden stick with a blunt end). Keep adding soil until it is one inch from the top of the container. Now pack the soil in place with your thumbs or a potting stick to eliminate air pockets. Do not pack too tightly or too loosely. Water plants thoroughly. For a few days keep plants in a fairly cool, bright place; in a week or so, after they have recovered from the shock of transplanting, move them to warmth and sun. You have to water hanging plants more frequently than plants at windows because, although they benefit from it, good air circulation also makes them dry out more quickly.

You may prefer to use two or three plants in a hanging container to get a better display in a short time. Arrange plants about two inches from the edges of the container—that is, toward the center of the pot.

Some excellent flowering plants for your gardens in the air are bougainvillaea and cascading petunias, nasturtiums and black-eyed Susans, all of which need a great deal of sun. For areas with less light—say, a west window—try Mexican love vine, ivy geraniums, morning glories, and passionflowers. In windows where light is moderate, use plants such as impatiens, campanulas, and fuchsias.

Plants at Levels

Group flowering plants along the walls of stairways to guide traffic and provide color. Along window walls, you may want to arrange a group to hide the sterile line where the wall meets the floor. Many homes and apartments have steps connecting rooms at different levels, and these are excellent places for potted plants.

Try potted bulbs (tulips, for example) at floor level in an entrance hall or at a focal point in a living room where guests enter, and they will immediately be greeted by a view of stunning color. Use many plants of a particular kind, never just one or two. To add some color and fill in bare areas around very large decorator plants, set pots of "mums" at floor level. Or try groups of caladiums. Caladiums are not really flowering plants, but their bright leaves are as pretty as flowers. The added color will bring dimension and interest to a room with little effort and cost. Low-growing primroses in cylindrical pots are especially pleasing at floor level, and in groups they provide a distinctive note. Agapanthus, a fine bulbous plant, is also very effective as a floor plant.

A very popular and useful interior designer's trick is to place potted flowering plants near a full-length window or door inside and again outside, so that a mirror effect is created. The colorful display visible indoors and outdoors at the same time makes the room seem larger.

If you have a garden room or area where you are growing many plants, by all means bring in the flowering plants to add color and variety. Use many pots of one kind of plant to create a concentration of color. A mix of different plants results in a spotty effect and does not make a handsome grouping.

Plants at Windows

The old-fashioned window garden is making a comeback, and there is more to this indoor garden than a few pots on the sill. First, you must decide on how to arrange the shelf space (discussed in Chapter 3) and the design of the window garden. Select, if possible, pots of the same color, so there is uniformity in the greenery. If you are using ornamental pots, choose the simple, elegant ones; too many designs can create a haphazard look.

For the most part, you will be limited to small plants (up to sixteen inches) at windows. Standard shelves cannot accommodate large pots, and usually the space between shelves is restricted to about twenty inches. Don't forget about window

There is a wealth of color in this room furnished by a concentration of gold chrysanthemums at floor level. (Photo by Max Eckert.)

Window greenhouses offer the gardener a way to have many garden flowers in the home to provide a pretty sight from indoors as well as outdoors. (Photo courtesy Lord & Burnham.)

returns (or recesses), where there is room for some hanging pots on bracket holders, and be sure to concentrate on a harmonious color composition. Monochromatic color schemes work well at windows; for example, pots of cyclamen in rose hues or orange nasturtiums and yellow marigolds make handsome combinations. If you prefer the cool colors, mix blue campanulas, for instance, with white flowering plants for an attractive look.

You will find a great number of good window plants in Chapter 6.

Flowers for Table, Desk, or Shelf

These are the areas where the solitary flowering plant in a decorative container is especially beautiful. But larger tables, desks, and shelves can "carry" the equally vivid impact of *many* potted flowering plants. Use long cachepots or containers for these bigger areas, grouping plants at the end of a dining table or the corner of a coffee table or hall desk to furnish color and add a different note to your home. When you arrange your table or desk groupings, always use flowers of the same color; remember, you want a concentration of brightness rather than a spotty effect. Flowering potted bulbs, such as zephyranthes and haemanthus, are beautiful on tables or desks and last for some time.

Flowering bulbs or potted plants are especially effective on shelves and in bookcases because they soften and beautify the hard sterile lines of the structure. The color is desirable, and the touch of grace a potted plant brings to an area is magnified when it is used in an unexpected place, such as a bookcase. Ideal flowering plants for this are azaleas, chrysanthemums, black-eyed Susans, cyclamen, nasturtiums, pepper plants, petunias and rainbow flowers.

Care

Remember to keep your indoor flowering plants watered and trimmed so they are well groomed. In most cases, plants can be

Chrysanthemums are lovely outdoors and just as desirable indoors
to decorate any area. (Photo by Matthew Barr.)

used as interior decoration for only a few days; then they should be returned to the window or to bright light to regain strength. Plants will suffer if left in interior locations too long, so move them back to their growing places after your guests have left.

Always keep pots and containers scrupulously clean when the plants are being used for decoration. At the window or other growing area a soiled pot may not be noticed, but in open locations they are always on display.

Provide suitable saucers under pots to prevent water from staining furniture. Do not forget that after a time even clay saucers will leave a water mark on tables, desks, or shelves, so remember to use cork mats under the saucers for extra protection.

ⴄᥬ ✿ ᥬⴄ

Growing Your Own Flowers

Annuals—which produce flowers, mature, and die in one season —provide quick color with excellent bloom the same year the plants are started. They are inexpensive and offer a great deal of satisfaction for the indoor gardener—it is a pity that most of these plants have been overlooked as house plants. Once started and in a sunny place, annuals need only water. Their bountiful gift of color will last for months.

Perennials are flowers that bloom year after year. They bloom either the first or second year after they are planted and outdoors live on for many years. However, indoors they are generally good only for one year. (Plants such as hollyhocks and pansies, which live only about two years, are known as biennials.) A table listing annuals and perennials is included at the end of this chapter. (See Chapter 6 for further descriptions.)

Bulbs are really indoor garden treasures because all you have to do is plant them; nature does the rest. The flowers, which are already in the bulbs, simply need light and moisture to bloom. Small planters of daffodils at windows offer a gay spot of color for little time and cost. (See Chapter 7 for descriptions of the various bulbs.)

Flowers grown indoors make beautiful floral arrangements. Here, one container has been slipped into another—in this case, a wicker basket. (Photo by Matthew Barr.)

Vines are either annual or perennial, and most are fast growers, making them ideal for indoor gardens. The flowering vines provide unbeatable green and gay color. It is best to start new plants each year. (Vines are fully covered in Chapter 8.)

From Seed

You can start most plants from seed or buy prestarted plants of, say, petunias in season (at nurseries). It is easy to grow your own plants by sowing seed, so we will tackle this method first.

Seed is available in packages from nurseries or mail-order suppliers. Growing plants from seed is the most economical way to have your own flowers indoors. Each packet contains many seeds, and the odds are all in your favor that some of them will grow and mature into lovely plants.

To start seed you will need some shallow containers, about four inches deep. Standard terra-cotta pots are fine for a *few* seeds. For *many* seeds, use plastic trays or the aluminum flats that frozen rolls come in. Cardboard milk cartons sliced lengthwise are fine for seed starting, too. You will need what is called a seed-starter medium, generally vermiculite or sand, which is sold at suppliers under various trade names. With all containers, make sure there are drainage holes, so excess moisture can escape. Otherwise, the starting medium will get waterlogged and seeds will not germinate.

Fill containers to ½ inch from the top with the starter mix; dampen the mix slightly. Now space seeds about one inch apart in the medium. Large seeds should be embedded to half their depth; small seeds can be scattered on top. Now carefully water the seeds with a spray or mister. Never just dump water into the container because this will wash away the seeds. If you like, you can buy one of the inexpensive tiny plastic greenhouses for seed starting. These are about twelve inches long and eight inches wide and have planting trays. Some come with heating cables to keep temperature constant and thus assure better germination.

Seed can be started from pellets or peat pots and later moved to pots of soil. Most annuals and perennials can be started in this way. (Photo by author.)

Here vermiculite is placed in a container for seed planting; note the tiny drain holes at sides. (Photo by Matthew Barr.)

(Heating cables are also available by themselves for homemade boxes.)

To sprout (germinate), seeds require warmth and good humidity. In the beginning bright light or even a shady place is fine. The top of a refrigerator is a good place to put seed containers because it is usually warm there (most seeds germinate at 70 to 7°F). To ensure good humidity, cover the containers with a sheet of glass or plastic Baggies propped on four sticks in tent fashion. If too much moisture condenses on the material, remove the covers for a few hours a day.

When seedlings start to sprout and show the second set of leaves, remove the cover and thin out the seedlings to give the strong ones more space to grow. Those you remove can be put into other containers or discarded. Then bring the plants into more light (at a window) and continue to keep the starter mix just moist, never soggy. When plants are two to three inches high, remove them from the seed container and plant them in suitable pots.

You can also start annuals and perennials in seed pellets or cubes (these are peat discs or cubes). The advantage of the pellet or cube is that there is less shock at transplanting time; you merely pot the entire peat ball.

From Prestarts

Prestarted annuals and perennials are available from nurseries in season. You can buy petunia prestarts that will bloom one week after you plant them. Of course, prestarts are more costly than starting your own, but they are conveniently past the crucial germination stage.

Prestarted plants come in plastic containers, generally six or twelve to a package. When you get them home, slice the soil, roots and all, as you would a cake, and with a small hand trowel gently remove each plant. Most of the starting mix will fall away, but do try, if at all possible, to keep the root ball intact.

Seeds are placed just below the surface of the starter mix. (Photo by Matthew Barr.)

Seeds are in place and the medium is moistened with a spray of water; a plastic tent will be placed over this to help provide humidity so seeds can germinate. (Photo by Matthew Barr.)

Prepare your pots or planters of fresh soil and put in the pre-started plants. Firm the soil around the collar of the plant and water well. Set the plants in a bright or sunny place. That is all there is to it.

Vines are started the same way as annuals and perennials.

Care of Seedlings

When your seedlings show their second set of leaves, they are ready for planting. To prepare your container for soil, cover the drainage holes with small patches of close-mesh screening or put a piece of pot shard over the holes. Then add a sprinkling of charcoal chips to keep the soil sweet and fill the box with soil to within ½ inch of the top to leave space for watering. No matter what kind of container you use or how large it is, do *not* bury the plants. Put your plants in place, laying out the roots in the soil. Firm the soil around the collar of the plant and pack it down firmly but not tightly. You want to eliminate air pockets in the soil, but you do not want to compact the soil so that air and water cannot enter it. Water thoroughly; let stand a few hours and then water again. Now place the container at a window or wherever the light is brightest. Sunlight is a necessity for a good crop of flowers, so seek out your sunniest place. Once the seedlings are established in their new home and growing, apply a packaged plant food. (See Chapter 2.)

Cuttings and Divisions

Seeds take time to germinate and sprout, but you can have plants in less time if you start from cuttings. A cutting is the section three to four inches from the top of a plant's stem, and you can plunk it into a jar of water or start it in vermiculite. The latter method is better for most cuttings because they need the starter mix to promote good root growth.

Use a household container, such as an aluminum frozen-cake tray or a plastic tray to start your cuttings. (Make sure any container has drainage holes in it.) Spread three to four inches of vermiculite in the bottom of the container. Dip the cut stems in rooting hormone (available at suppliers) and put them into the growing medium. Because cuttings have a better chance to grow with adequate humidity, make a plastic tent on sticks (see p. 50). The tent traps the moisture.

Now water the medium, but do not keep it sopping wet. Put the cuttings in a warm (75F), shady place for a few weeks. Then remove cuttings to see if roots have formed. If they have, transfer the plants to a three-inch pot of soil. If roots have not formed, replace the cuttings and wait.

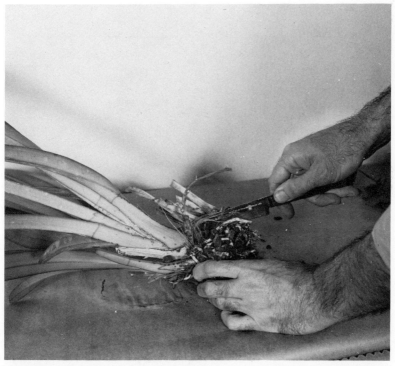

Here a mature plant is being divided to make two plants. (Photo by Matthew Barr.)

Any plant with multiple stems can—when it is mature—be divided to make two or more plants. Division is simply pulling apart a large plant, roots and all, to make new plants, and you can do this by hand—gently—or better yet, use a knife and sever the plant in two. Start the new plant in vermiculite or put it directly into a pot of soil and keep it warm and moist for a month while it regains vigor. Then repot in a larger container of fresh soil and grow it as you would any plant.

List of Annuals and Perennials

Botanical and Common Name	Optimum Temperature for Seed Germination	Weeks Required for Seed to Germinate
Browallia	70–75	1–2
Calendula (pot marigold)	68–70	2–3
Campanula (bellflower)	68–86	2–3
Chrysanthemum	68–70	2–4
Dimorphotheca (cape marigold)	68–70	2–3
Felicia (blue marguerite)	65–70	1–2
Gazania	68–72	2–3
Impatiens	68–70	2–4
Lathyrus (sweet pea)	68–86	2–3
Petunia	68–70 (some varieties need higher temperatures)	2–3

Botanical and Common Name	Optimum Temperature for Seed Germination	Weeks Required for Seed to Germinate
Primula (primrose)	45–50	2–4
Tagetes (marigold)	68–86	1–2
Tropaeolum (nasturtium)	68–70	1–3

See Chapter 6 for more specific information on these plants.

ｄ৯ ✿ ৎﾑ

Nasturtiums
at Your Window

The following plant résumés include some annuals and perennials, as well as some shrubs to decorate your home. If you have
never considered these plants as indoor subjects, do so, because
most of them are fine at windows. Some do not last for years, but
they will certainly last many months (petunias, for example).
And remember that most garden flowers can be harvested inex-
pensively: for $10 you can have an abundance of blooms.

Some of the following plants are a bit tricky to start indoors,
but none is impossible. It is simply a matter of potting them in
good soil, feeding them every so often, and most important, making sure they get plenty of water. Garden flowers, more than
any other type of plant, require ample moisture to do their thing.

Most of the plants will do just fine at a south or east window.
The harvest will not be as plentiful indoors as it would be in the
garden, but you will get enough flowers to use in vases or as
decorations for tables, desks, or windows. There is genuine re-
ward in growing these indoor/outdoor plants in your home.

Acalypha (Chenille Plant)

Acalyphas are fine indoor subjects, with their handsome broad, ovate leaves and dense, dramatic, red pendant spikes. The chenille plant is always handsome in pretty little cachepots and requires little care—just a bright location and water about three times a week. My plant (from a prestart) bloomed in August and was still in color in December. The plants can be started from seed, and they root so easily from cuttings that this is the best way to multiply your supply.

The species to try are *A. godseffiana* and *A. hispida*, both available at most nurseries. The plants are certainly worth space at your window and add a great deal of charm indoors. Little effort is required; even the brown thumber can grow them.

Althaea (Hollyhock)

If you have always admired those pretty giant hollyhocks outdoors, you can now have them in dwarf form indoors. These plants grow to about thirty-six inches. Hollyhocks, tall and with figlike leaves, are not especially handsome as pot plants, but they bear splendid wide-faced red, yellow or orange flowers in summer, which are magnificent cut flowers. Grow the plants in deep containers (at least twelve inches) and get ready for a lovely display.

If you start seeds in early June or buy prestarted plants, they will generally bloom the same year. Sun and lots of water are necessary to make hollyhocks do their best.

The two species of garden hollyhocks are *A. rosea* and *A. ficifolia*, but for indoors specify the dwarf variety that is now available from mail-order suppliers.

Ardisia (Coral Plant)

These showy outdoor plants do just as well indoors. They have rose-colored flowers, dark green leaves, and best of all, bright red berries in brilliant drooping clusters that last for weeks. They have been overlooked for indoor decoration.

Ardisias can be started from seed or from plants bought at nurseries. Use porous soil because drainage is essential to produce healthy plants. Water copiously all year (these plants really like water). Bright light is fine all year, except in summer, when light shading is required. Grow the plants at 65F during spring and summer and 55F the rest of the year. Do not feed them because this can prevent berries from forming.

After a few years ardisias get somewhat leggy, so take cuttings for new plants rather than try to carry old ones over. *A. crenata* is the most popular species.

Azalea (Rhododendron)

These vibrantly colored flowering gems always make stunning gift plants. The variety 'Gumpo', which is a smaller type of azalea, is generally available at florists in January; the flowers may be red or white. The plants have a nice branching habit, are neither too small nor too large, and look handsome displayed in ornamental pottery almost anyplace in the home.

When you get your azaleas, put them in a bright but not sunny place that is about 65F. Keep the soil evenly moist, and mist the leaves occasionally. As the flowers fade (in about four or five weeks), reduce watering to allow the plants to rest. When warm weather starts (usually in May), first cut the plants back somewhat (leave about six inches of stem) and then put them outside on a porch or window sill. Repot, resume regular watering, and start a mild feeding program. In early September move

This azalea has had fine care; it is symmetrical in shape and full of flowers. The azalea needs lots of water and bright light. (Photo courtesy California Association of Nurserymen.)

the plants indoors to a cool place and increase heat and water as the months go by. The plants should start showing buds around Christmas.

Treat azaleas the same the second year as you did the first, but use a larger pot. Watch out for red spider mites. If you see the webs of these pests or silver streaks on the leaves, use proper remedies. (See Chapter 9.)

Brodiaea (Spring Starflower)

Brodiaeas are bulbous plants, but they are rarely listed as such, which is why they are included in this general section. These plants are desirable because of the clusters of pale blue, or yellow-tinged purple, funnel-shaped blooms they bear atop their wiry stems. They are really quite handsome.

Grow several to a pot for a good display. Use a somewhat sandy soil, and give brodiaeas good sunlight all year. A moderate temperature—say, 65F—suits them. When the plants die down, dry them gradually and store them for the next year. In attractive containers brodiaeas make excellent indoor decoration, so do try them.

There are a couple of species available: *B. ixioides* and *B. uniflora*, and recently some fine varieties have developed. This is a very unusual and good indoor/outdoor plant, even for the novice.

Browallia

These annuals are superb because of their vivid blue or violet flowers. The plants have an airy look, grow to about two feet, and are right at home in your home. Native to South America, browallias will grace your window sill for many months, and they can be started from seed indoors or purchased as prestarts.

Give the plants a rich soil with plenty of water. A bright window will suit them, although some sunlight is fine, too. After blooming, which generally lasts from August through October, you must discard the plants because they are good for only a season.

Browallias can also be used in hanging eight- or ten-inch baskets. For a spectacular display, group several plants in an ornamental container and use as a table or desk piece. This is a plant that has been overlooked but that can really impress visitors—and you, too. Select *B. americana*, sometimes sold as *B. alata*, or *B. viscosa* and *B. speciosa*. *B. major* is too large for indoors.

Brunfelsia (Yesterday, Today, and Tomorrow Plant)

Brunfelsia, with its small flat-faced blue flowers, is especially pleasing because it has such a lovely scent.

Many people have told me that this shrub is difficult to grow, but if you give it good care, it will prosper and do very well indoors. Grow the plants in a rich, loose soil at 75F. Give them some sunlight in winter, but keep them shaded in summer. Brunfelsias can grow quite large once they get going, and they will need a ten-inch pot when mature. Keep the soil evenly moist, and do remember to feed biweekly because this heavy feeder will not bloom without additional food.

B. calycina generally blooms from fall to spring and is a delight at the window in winter, when color may be scarce in the indoor garden.

Calendula (Pot Marigold)

I buy pots of these bright garden annuals at nurseries and keep them growing at my windows as long as possible. The colors of the flowers are so vibrant—bright oranges and yellows—that they are especially worth the space. Calendulas make fine cut flowers

CALENDULA

—another reason for having them indoors. It's nice to snip your own fresh blooms for indoor decoration.

Keep the soil quite moist and put calendulas at a sunny window. Or use the plants throughout the house to furnish bright color so often needed in rooms—at floor level, on tables, and so forth. Remove spent flowers to prolong bloom.

Campanula (Bellflower)

This large group of annuals and perennials have delightful blue or violet flowers in a variety of hues. The leaves are small, pretty, and generally scalloped, and the plants have a fine bushy habit.

A well-grown plant is a desirable addition to any room, and surprisingly, campanulas do quite well indoors because they require only a bright spot, not intense sunlight. Coolness (55F) is of prime importance in maturing a healthy specimen. The plants can be started from seed indoors, or small plants can be purchased at seasonal times during the year. Generally, campanulas bloom for a long time. The perennial types will bloom, die down for a few months, and then start to grow again. Keep the plants cool and moist.

Because there are so many species, it is hard to say which are best for indoors. I find the perennial *C. elatines* quite successful; it is low-growing (to about twelve inches), with fine blue flowers. *C. fragilis* is vinelike, with blue blooms, and *C. isophylla* with its saucer-shaped blue flowers, makes an excellent hanging plant. White-flowered forms are also available, usually designated as *C. alba*.

Capsicum (Pepper Plant)

This handsome small plant appears in winter in florist shops. The pretty green leaves and bright red fruit make it a desirable addition to any home. The berries, or peppers, are green at first, turning red as the days grow shorter. They are edible but extremely hot.

A tropical shrub from South America, the pepper plant requires warmth (78F) and copious water to be at its best. Generally, the plant, an annual, will be good only for a season, but it is a long season, lasting from October well into February. Frequently it will live from year to year—and mine is in its second year. In late winter I trimmed it back radically, repotted it, and then kept it in a cool place, watering it just enough to keep the soil from caking. As the weather warmed, I increased moisture and light and temperature (to 75F), and the plant sprouted fresh growth.

The pepper plant is a handsome indoor plant, and there are many varieties available. *Note:* do not confuse this plant with the related *Solanum pseudo-capsicum,* known as the Jerusalem cherry.

Celosia (Cockscomb)

This annual grows best in a hot, sunny window, where the red flower clusters (resembling a cockscomb) will stay in color for many weeks. The plant grows to about twenty-four inches and makes a fine indoor subject; it is of further value because the flowers can be used for drying, as well as for cut flowers. Keep the soil evenly moist at all times and provide feeding every other watering.

Celosias are available at nurseries, generally as prestarts, and require only planting to get them growing well. Or you can buy mature plants. The flowers are not very dramatic, but the plants do so well indoors, I suggest you try them. Also, they are inexpensive. Celosias only last one season.

Celosia plumosa is a highly desirable plant because it bears red flower spikes that last a long time and is easy to grow. (Photo by author.)

Chrysanthemum

There are chrysanthemums and chrysanthemums—all kinds and all sizes—enough to boggle the mind. The potted chrysanthemums you see at florists in fall and winter can be grown quite successfully indoors for some time.

C. frutescens and its varieties are the best chrysanthemums. The flowers vary in shape and color, but all seem to be very floriferous if they are in a cool, bright place and have plenty of water. After the plants bloom, cut them down to about two inches and move them to a frost-free garage or pantry. Give them occasional waterings; they will start re-growth in spring. Place the chrysanthemums at windows in pots of fresh soil and start watering for a new harvest of flowers. *C. frutescens* is a hardy perennial, so you can have flowers years after year.

Grow masses of chrysanthemums for the windows in large bins, say, eight inches deep, or simply group them in six-or eight-inch-deep pots, and hide the rims of the pots under a layer of sphagnum moss.

Dimorphotheca (Cape Marigold)

I grow these outdoors because I love the large, daisylike yellow flowers and tall stems, but I also grow them indoors in pots.

Indoors, the plants grow to thirty-six inches and seem to do well in any type of soil as long as they get plenty of water and sun. Feed at every other watering, but decrease moisture when buds open. Use three or four plants in a six-inch pot and keep rather cool (55F).

Just ask for dimorphotheca at nurseries; there are several good varieties, and all seem to be very robust.

MINIATURE CHRYSANTHEMUM

Felicia (Blue Marguerite)

Do not envy your neighbor who grows these lovely blue daisies outdoors; you can have them indoors in containers at a sunny window. The best part about felicias is that they bloom through the winter and add great cheer indoors. The plants never exceed twelve inches, so they are perfect house plants if space is a problem.

This South African plant needs a standard soil and a heavy supply of moisture at all times. Feed at every other watering. Make new plants each year from cuttings.

The botanical name is *F. amelloides,* and there are many good varieties.

Fuchsia (Lady's Eardrop)

Fuchsias are the cascading plants so often seen in shady gardens, where they bloom profusely. For pot culture they are best grown in hanging baskets at a western exposure. The plants have a flush of growth in spring, followed by a harvest of bloom and then a rest for several months before the cycle is repeated.

Grow fuchsias in a sandy soil and keep them well watered in the growing season. After the blooms have faded, allow the soil to dry out somewhat and keep the plants only moist, never wet. Place them in cooler locations, about 55F. In early spring increase watering and give the plants more light and warmth; cut them back to about five or six inches, allowing strong shoots to remain; this encourages new growth. Repot the plants in fresh soil, increase watering, and give more light and warmth. Always keep fuchsias trimmed and groomed by pinching off dead flowers and wan stems, so there is good symmetry.

There are so many varieties, it is impossible to suggest specific types; study mail-order catalogs and select those with colors you prefer.

FELICIA

Fuchsias are lovely indoor plants for bright, but not sunny, places; they are very floriferous and come in many varieties one more colorful than the other. (Photo by author.)

Gazania

These favorite annuals are valued for their yellow, orange, or scarlet blooms. The plants rarely grow to more than eight inches, so they are perfect house plants.

Use a rich, sharp draining soil because gazanias will not tolerate a stale one. The plants are very floriferous if grown in good sun, but cool (55F), and they need buckets of water. For a really good display, grow many gazanias in shallow tubs. Buy prestarts in season, grow your own from seed, or take divisions of plants from the garden.

There are many gazanias available, but perhaps G. *splendens* and several improved varieties are the most popular.

Impatiens

These lovely garden flowers have been perfected by hybridists, so there are now many varieties. The flat, open-faced flowers are red, white, or pink. The plants are especially floriferous and in the home will provide a mass of color from July to October or beyond. Most of the plants sold now are bushy, robust, and excellent.

Impatiens are perfect for the home because they do not require excessive sunlight and can bear flowers at a bright window. But they do need plenty of water and moderate feeding. Grow impatiens in tubs or pots about ten inches across and replenish them yearly. Impatiens also look handsome in hanging baskets; trim and clip them as desired to create a halo of color.

There are several types of impatiens. For best indoor/outdoor use, try varieties such as I. 'Elfin' and the spectacular I. 'Red Ruby,' both with dark green, almost black leaves and vivid red flowers.

A favorite garden flower, impatiens, grows well indoors because it needs only bright light to bear flowers. (Photo by author.)

Lantana

If lantana has always struck you as an outdoor plant, consider it now as an indoor flowering beauty. It does remarkably well at windows and can put on quite a show in late fall months, when color is so much wanted. The species *L. camara* bears orange flower clusters, and *L. montevidensis* (my favorite) has lavender blooms.

LANTANA

Lantana is a sprawler and thus needs some room to be at its best. Lantana likes a very moist soil and a bright location, but sunlight is not necessary for bloom. Start the plants from seed or cuttings (they grow quickly).

L. camara will bloom during summer, but *L. montevidensis* (trailing lantana) can bloom almost all winter if given routine care. Put it into a hanging basket for maximum effect.

Pelargonium (Geranium)

These festive plants offer almost constant color if given full sun and grown rather cool, with frequent airing and plenty of space at windows. The family is so vast that it is difficult to suggest specifically which kind of geranium to grow, but there is a choice of zonals, standard types, carefree types, dwarfs, 'Martha Washington' varieties, and the scented-leaf geraniums.

Whichever you choose, grow geraniums in a slightly acid soil (see Chapter 2); this is one time it pays to take the time to test the soil in the pot with a soil-testing kit. An acid soil should be about 6.5 to 7.0. Water the plants freely and then allow them to dry out somewhat before watering again. Geraniums bloom best when pot-bound, so grow the plants in small pots. The 'Martha Washington' and scented types tend to rest in winter, so water them moderately then and do not feed. Feed all other types once a month when the plants are in active growth—that is, most of the time in sunny conditions. Avoid overwatering geraniums, and be sure the humidity is not too high.

Petunia

These wonderful annual garden flowers are just as lovely indoors. The plants are very floriferous, and there are a number of varieties; the trailing types especially are handsome at a win-

A bower of cascading geraniums to please any eye. (Photo by author.)

Outdoor beauty comes indoors with a container of petunias; these are well-grown plants with an abundance of bloom. Ample sun and water does it. (Photo courtesy Pan American Seed Co.)

dow. Growth is somewhat straggly, and leaves are not handsome, but the large funnel-shaped flowers come in an array of colors, including deep red and violet.

Petunias are easy to grow: start your own from seed, or buy prestarts at nurseries in season. Petunias require a rich soil (see Chapter 2), buckets of water, and feeding every other watering. Some plants will die down in the middle of summer and then have another crop of flowers in fall.

Primula (Primrose)

These perky little plants come in a dazzling array of colors and are available in season at nurseries. They are instant color for the window garden, and while they do not last a long time indoors, they are worth the space. The plants require buckets of water and a sunny location and just as they are used in gardens for bright accent areas, they can be part of the indoor flower farm.

You can start seed or, as mentioned, buy plants already in bloom at suppliers. There are dozens of varieties, so choose the colors you like best and enjoy primroses indoors.

Raphiolepis (Indian Hawthorn)

This delightful evergreen plant bears abundant star-shaped pink flowers. Grow the shrub in well-drained soil in a large tub. Water heavily through the summer, but not so much the rest of the year. Give the plant a bright location, and feed it every two weeks in warm weather, once a month the rest of the year. Trim and prune the bush to keep it in a handsome shape. You might even try this plant in topiary fashion.

Indian hawthorn is available under the name *R. indica.*

Tagetes (Marigold)

Native to Argentina, marigolds (from the Compositae family) are annual herbs, with dissected leaves and solitary or clustered heads of orange or red flowers. These floriferous plants can be grown easily indoors and will provide abundant bloom all summer. They are excellent cut flowers and last for weeks.

Not as temperamental as petunias or nasturtiums, marigolds can tolerate a dry soil, but they do need ample sun to produce their lovely blooms.

The botanical name is *T. signata* or *tenuifolia*, and there are dozens of varieties. The French marigold *T. patula* is also available, but it's best to stay with the small or miniature varieties, which do not grow over twenty-four inches.

Tropaeolum (Nasturtium)

These fast-growing herbs with their vividly colored flowers—orange, yellow, red—are well known in the garden, and their splashy colors brighten any area. The plants are graceful and dramatic, and their dark leaves make a handsome foil for the bright flowers. Most of the species are climbing or trailing, and when grown in pots, they can be used as hanging plants or simply as room accents—on desks or tables or, better yet, at windows where they really show off.

Nasturtiums do well in a sandy soil and can be started from seed sown directly into the soil. They like plenty of water and good, bright light. As a window plant, nasturtiums can grow almost all year, blooming off and on through the months. Pick off dead leaves (which are natural) and faded blooms as they appear. Eventually, the plants will spend themselves and must be replaced with new plants.

The common garden species is *T. majus*, which has several varieties. *T. pentaphyllum*, a definite climber, and the vermillion *T. speciosum*, from Chile, are other good nasturtiums. Because these plants do so well indoors, try a few different species and enjoy them to the fullest.

List of Plants

Botanical and Common Name	Height, in Inches	Color	Bloom Season	Remarks
Acalypha godseffiana (chenille plant)	36–48	greenish yellow	spring, summer	good indoors
A. hispida	36–48	red	summer	excellent color
Althaea ficifolia (hollyhock)	60	lemon yellow	summer, fall	a favorite
A. rosea	30	most colors	summer	a favorite
Ardisia crenata (coral plant)	20	red (berries)	fall	nice accent

Botanical and Common Name	Height, in Inches	Color	Bloom Season	Remarks
Azalea	24	red	spring	fine color
Brodiaea ixioides (spring starflower)	18	salmon, yellow	spring, summer	pretty
B. uniflora	8	white	summer	pretty
Browallia americana (*alata*)	24	violet	summer	always good
B. speciosa	16	blue	summer	always good
B. viscosa	18	blue, white	summer	always good
Brunfelsia calycina (yesterday, today, and tomorrow plant)	30	purple	summer	good color
Calendula (pot marigold)	24	yellow, orange	summer	floriferous
Campanula elatines (bellflower)	20	blue	spring to fall	good basket plant
C. fragilis	20	white	spring to fall	very pretty
C. isophylla	20	blue	spring to fall	large flowers
Capsicum annum (pepper plant)	30	red (peppers)	fall	oddity
Celosia (cockscomb)	24	red	summer	easy to grow
Chrysanthemum frutescens	28	many colors	summer, fall	fine plant
Dimorphotheca (cape marigold)	16	yellow	late summer	good in pots
Felicia amelloides (blue marguerite)	24	blue	spring, summer	stellar color

Botanical and Common Name	Height, in Inches	Color	Bloom Season	Remarks
Fuchsia (lady's eardrop)	30	many colors	spring	good basket plant
Gazania splendens	14	many colors	summer	a running
Impatiens 'Elfin'	12	red	summer, fall	one of the best
I. 'Red Ruby'	12	scarlet	fall	one of the best
Lantana camara	30	pink	summer	easy
L. montevidensis (trailing lantana)	30	lavender	spring	easy
Pelargonium (geranium)	30	many colors	spring, summer	a favorite
Petunia	20	all colors except blue	summer	many varieties
Primula (primrose)	16	many colors	spring	bright color
Raphiolepis indica (Indian hawthorn)	48	pink	summer	nice shrub
Tagetes patula (marigold)	18	yellow, orange	fall	floriferous
T. signata	20	yellow, orange	summer	good in pots
Tropaeolum majus (nasturtium)	18	yellow, orange	summer, fall	my favorite
T. pentaphyllum	20	yellow, orange	summer, fall	good
T. speciosum	trailer	yellow, orange	summer, fall	nice viner

[CHAPTER 7]

❦ ✿ ❧

Bulbs

Bulbous plants are nature's way of making gardeners out of non-gardeners. Outdoors you just put bulbs into the ground and leave them to produce a bountiful harvest of flowers. Indoors you put them into pots of soil and again, just enjoy them (although inside, bulbs do not produce so bountiful a crop). Bulbs are easy to grow because they already contain all necessary food for the year's flowers. All you do is add water; nature does the rest. Containers of blooming bulbs at the windows brighten dull winter days (there are numerous bulbs that bloom in the gray season), and many can be carried over from year to year.

The secret of growing bulbs (if there is one) is to start them slowly, with moderate watering, and then increase moisture as the leaves start to grow. Biweekly feedings with a mild plant food (10-10-5) and a pinch of bone meal guarantee bloom. A rich soil with some sand (see Chapter 2) suits most bulbs; drainage is vital with these plants.

Most people are a little confused about which end of the bulb goes into the growing medium and how far it should be embedded, so I have included this information in the following plant résumés. Some of the plants in the list may be unknown to you because they are not grown much by home gardeners. Yet they should be tried—many are positively beautiful. Some of these little-known bulbs will be easy to locate, and others will be somewhat difficult, but all are worth the search.

Plants that grow from corms (smaller than bulbs) and from tuberous roots and rhizomes (longer and narrower than bulbs) are included within the bulb classification that follows.

Achimenes (Rainbow Flower)

Achimenes, related to gloxinias, have to be started from rhizomes because they are not available as potted plants. The flowers come in many colors, depending on the variety—all are beautiful and worth having.

Start the rhizomes in late winter or early spring, covering them with about one inch of soil, place in warmth (78F), and keep them uniformly moist. Give achimenes warm sun, and plenty of water when they are putting forth blooms. After the flowers fade, reduce watering and let the rhizomes dry off gradually (for about five weeks). Store them in a cool (60F) place for about three months and then start them again.

Grow several rhizomes to a pot for a good display. For a succession of blooms, start some plants in February and follow up with another crop in about six weeks. This way, you will have flowers at your windows for many months.

Agapanthus (Lily of the Nile)

This is a favorite outdoor flower on the West Coast, and the newer miniature varieties are excellent for indoor growing. Tuberous-rooted, agapanthuses bear flowers in midsummer—lovely white or blue florets, dozens to a cluster.

The plants require roomy tubs; start them slightly beneath the surface in a sandy soil and keep them in a light, sunny place

AGAPANTHUS

where it is about 70F. Keep the soil evenly moist at all times while the plant is making growth and through the bloom season. After the flowers fade, provide just enough water to keep the leaves from falling and grow them barely moist through the winter. If possible, move the plants to a cool (55F) location. In spring give them more light and warmth and keep the soil almost wet. In active growth these plants can take plenty of water.

The best varieties for indoors are *A. orientalis* 'Dwarf White' and 'Peter Pan.'

Caladium

Outdoors or indoors, these are the fancy-leafed, beautifully colored plants that everyone wants—and there are so many new varieties, the choice of colors is staggering. The lance-shaped leaves are large, and the plants grow to about thirty inches.

Between February and April, plant caladium tubers one inch below a rich soil (see Chapter 2) and give them good warmth (78F) and moisture to promote growth. Fertilize monthly with 10-10-5 plant food until the weather starts to turn cool (about September) and then allow the plants to dry out somewhat and do not give any food. Let foliage mature and dry off so the plants can go through their rest from October through February. Keep them in pots in a shady, dry place at a temperature of about 55F. In the spring, repot the tubers in fresh soil for another season of beauty.

Crinum

Crinum is a fine bulb often overlooked for indoor growing. It produces lilylike pink or red flowers from April to July.

Plant one bulb in a ten-inch pot; leave the tip of the bulb above the surface of a rich soil that contains some sphagnum.

Good drainage is essential for these amaryllis, so put gravel at the bottom of the pot. Start plants in late fall and water scantily until growth starts; then increase moisture and feed once every two weeks. Give plants bright light but never intense sun and keep them cool at night (55F). They can be rested and started again each year, but they can also be grown all year. Repot every four years.

There are numerous crinums, including *C.* 'Ellen Bousanquet,' *C. giganteum,* and *C. moorei.*

Crocus

You will find crocuses blooming in gardens in early spring, and indoor types bloom in the fall as well. With their lovely small blue flowers on short stems, these delightful plants offer fine color for the indoor garden and are so easy to bloom; some of them even burst into flower without being planted.

But that is no way to treat a crocus; instead, start five or six corms in a seven-inch container of gravel or sand and soil. Leave the tips showing. Water moderately for a few weeks and then increase moisture and warmth. Keep the plants cool at night (50F). The blooms last a few weeks and add beauty to any area; after they fade, you must discard them, for they are not permanent plants.

You can also buy crocuses at florists already planted in containers and ready to bloom if you want to do it the fast way, but that really takes all the fun out of it. *C. zonatus* is the species name.

Cyclamen

Cyclamens flower in rich hues from reds to magentas to vibrant pinks, and they always remind me of shooting stars.

Place six or eight corms, with the pointed tips up, about

Crocuses grown in pots indoors provide a flush of color in their season. (Photo Wayside Gardens.)

½ inch below the soil. Use a rich, friable growing medium (see Chapter 2). Start the plant slowly—that is, with only bright light and even moisture—and when growth is started, move them to a warm but never hot place with more light and increase moisture. If you buy a cyclamen plant already in bloom (and now they are available almost year-round at florists), simply reduce moisture after it has finished blooming and move it to a cool place, then grow it very dry for a few months. When you want to bring plants to bloom again, repot the corms in fresh soil and increase moisture and warmth.

The Amazon lily is amenable to potting. Its dark green leaves and crystal-white flowers make a welcome addition to the window garden. (Photo by author.)

Eucharis (Amazon Lily)

This is one of my favorite bulb plants—you cannot go wrong with it. The Amazon lily bears clusters of fragrant white flowers on twelve-inch stems and has attractive large green leaves. Eucharis generally flowers in spring or summer, but mine once bloomed in winter.

The plant definitely needs periods of growth and then rest (when less water is required), with 60F temperatures. Cover the bulbs to about half their depth and use a coarse, fibrous soil (see Chapter 2). Water sparingly until growth starts, but always keep the soil somewhat moist. Warm temperatures (70 to 80F) will encourage the bulbs to sprout, and the plants require good sun all year. Use the Amazon lily as a pot plant only; do not cut flowers. A stellar indoor/outdoor plant.

E. grandiflora is available from suppliers as bulbs, although occasionally small plants are also available.

Eucomis (Pineapple Lily)

This plant is almost never grown outdoors, so why grow it indoors? First, because it is an exquisite flowering gem, and second, because it does so well in pot culture. This bulb has bright green, strap-shaped leaves and a thick stalk adorned with dozens of tiny whitish green flowers. Eucomis is a truly unique plant; the rosettes of leaves resemble pineapple foliage—thus the common name.

Plant the bulbs in fall, just below the surface of soil; use a sandy soil mix (see Chapter 2). Water scantily until February; then increase moisture. Keep the plant in a shady location until the leaves start growing and then move it into the light. For best results, grow at a night temperature of 50F, and keep the plant in the same pot (ten- or twelve-inch) for several years without repotting. This outdoor lily can make you an indoor gardener.

The best species for indoors are *E. punctata* and *E. undulata.*

Gloriosa (Glory Lily)

This bulbous plant, which grows outdoors in tropical climates, can do beautifully indoors as a pot plant. This is a climbing lily with an exotic red and yellow flower.

Plant the long, slender tuber in the fall. Place one tuber just below the surface of a sandy soil (see Chapter 2) in an eight-inch pot and water moderately until the leaves show. Then increase moisture. When the leaves turn yellow, store the tubers dry until the following fall. The plants need rather warm temperatures (60F) and bright but not sunny light.

G. *rothschildiana*, the most popular of the group, is usually available in packages at florist or novelty stores.

Haemanthus (Blood Lily)

This spring- or fall-flowering amaryllis from South Africa was made for indoor culture. The flower head is produced on top of a stout stem, and the ball of blooms may contain 100 or more tiny red flowers—quite a sight! The blood lily is a spectacular pot plant for room accent; do not use it as cut flowers.

The bulbs are large, so use one to an eight-inch pot; pot firmly in a rich, rapidly draining soil, with the top ½ inch of the bulb protruding. Start the bulbs in the fall, with just scant moisture, but water well after growth appears. Feed every other week with mild liquid fertilizer. In summer some shading is necessary, but during the rest of the year, the plant thrives on sunshine.

H. *katherinae* is one of the finest reds, and it blooms in spring after the foliage ripens. It is evergreen and needs no storage. H. *multiflorus* generally blooms first and then produces foliage. The plant is dormant during winter. H. *coccineus* grows all winter but is dormant in summer. During their dormant periods, these blood lilies should be kept cool (50F) and fairly dry, away from the light.

Hyacinthus (Hyacinth)

Hyacinths bear large plumes with hundreds of tiny flowers; the colors are white, pink, or blue. You can buy them in pots or glass jars (in October or November) at florists. Or you can start your own bulbs. To do this, use three or four bulbs to a six-

HAEMANTHUS

HYACINTH

or seven-inch pot, with the necks protruding slightly above the soil line. After potting, keep the bulbs in a shady, cool (50F) place—perhaps a basement or garage. When the top growth is four or five inches high (in about eight weeks), move the bulbs to light and warmth. You can also start hyacinths in water in special glass vases (then handle as described above).

When buying hyacinth bulbs, ask for indoor types. You can also buy plants already started from florists. In any case, the plants are good only for a season.

Ixia (African Corn Lily)

With their lovely, small funnel-shaped flowers and grassy foliage, ixias are common outdoor flowers that give much color indoors, but they *must* be grown cool (45F). The flowers are white, pink, red, or yellow.

Start six or eight corms in a ten-inch pot of soil in fall and cover them with straw. Then place the pot outdoors on a porch or balcony until December. Water the corms twice a month while outdoors, but when you take them in, start watering more and place the plants in full sunlight. Glorious indoor blooms should start in four to six weeks. After they finish blooming, store the bulbs in the same pot covered with a paper sack in a cool, dry place until the following August. Then repot for a new season of bloom.

I. maculata is yellow; *I. speciosa* is red. There are many named varieties.

Lachenalia (Cape Cowslip)

These bulbs from South Africa have pink to red or orange or violet flowers; the bells appear on a tall scape.

Use a six- or eight-inch pot and cram in a dozen or more bulbs about *an inch below the soil.* Start the plants in September and be sure you use a quick-draining medium. Water after planting and set the pots outdoors (45F) on a porch or balcony until early December. Then bring them into the home and increase watering, but still maintain cool temperatures (55F). Give the plants sun and feed them every second watering. After the flowers fade, let the foliage ripen naturally, then store the bulbs in pots covered with paper bags in a cool dark place. In September repot in fresh soil.

L. tricolor varieties are the most popular and readily available.

Lycoris (Spider Lily)

This amaryllis from China and Japan bears large and striking orange flowers on thirty-six-inch stalks and is quite a sight indoors. Blooms appear in late fall or winter when the foliage starts to die off. Lycoris is a difficult bulb to find but this magnificent flowering plant is well worth the search.

In fall or winter plant single bulbs in loose soil in six-inch pots, with the nose of the bulb just above the surface. Start them slowly with little water, progressing to moderate waterings and finally to a good deal of moisture. Give the plants full sunshine to promote heavy blooming and repot only when necessary (these plants can go three or four years without being disturbed).

The only available species is *L. aurea.*

Narcissus (Paperwhites)

These favorite flowering bulbs, generally called paperwhites, have a lovely fragrance and are very easy to grow.

Several bulbs can be started in a shallow container filled with gravel; embed the bulbs so the tops protrude about ½ inch above the surface. Place the container in a cool (60F), shady location and keep the gravel moist. Move it to a warm, sunny place at the

NARCISSUS

window when the leaves are four to five inches high. The plants will bear flowers in a few weeks.

Narcissus are good only for the season. Yet, even for their short time in flower, they are worthwhile because they are easy to grow and so lovely. *N. tazetta* is the indoor white narcissus, and *N. soleil d'or* is the splendid yellow.

Ornithogalum (Star-of-Bethlehem)

I am especially partial to ornithogalums because they make such fine cut flowers. Many white or yellow blooms come from a leafless stalk in winter when color is scarce at windows. Once planted, ornithogalums are really quite easy to grow, and they should be in every window garden. They bear a wealth of flowers that last several weeks and make a stellar indoor accent.

Plant six or seven bulbs in an eight-inch pot, one inch below the soil surface. From September to November keep the bulbs cool (60F), and when growth starts increase moisture, warmth, and light. Give plenty of water. After blooming is over, keep the foliage growing and let the bulbs dry off gradually. Then store them in the same pots in a cool (55F), shaded place until the following season.

Several species are available: *O. arabicum* is white with a greenish eye; *O. thyrsoides* is white with a brown center; and *O. aureum* is a fine yellow.

Oxalis

Most people regard these flowering gems as weeds and pull them from their gardens. But oxalis plants are delightful, tiny plants with white, yellow, or red flowers, and some of them bloom off and on throughout the year.

Plant three or four corms in the fall in an eight-inch pot of rich soil. Push the corms into the soil about ½ inch. Keep the soil scantily watered until growth starts, and then increase moisture. Feed twice a month with fertilizer that contains some bone meal. If you want flowers from these beauties, give them ample sunlight. The summer and fall varieties (your nurseryman can tell you which) require a rest in winter with little water. Replant the corms in fresh soil every year.

A partial list of oxalis includes *O. bowicama*, red, *O. vermua*, bright yellow; *O. hirta*, rose-pink; *O. rubra*, veined rose.

Sprekelia (Jacobean Lily)

Sometimes called an amaryllis, sprekelia is a plant that bears a magnificent crimson bloom on a tall stem. It is a dramatic flower.

Blossoming occurs six to eight weeks after planting. Pot the bulbs with their necks just above the soil in seven- or eight-inch pots (use two or three bulbs to a pot). Keep them in a warm, shady place until growth shows and then transfer to a bright but cool (65F) window. Be sure the soil is evenly moist at all times, and after blooming is over, let the foliage ripen naturally. Then dry it out somewhat during the rest period and return it to cooler (55F) temperatures. In a few months repot in fresh soil and start the growing cycle again.

This truly spectacular bulb is sold as *S. formosissima* and is sometimes called Jacobean lily or Aztec lily.

Tulbaghia (Society Garlic)

This is a terrible name for a lovely plant that bears clusters of lavender flowers. Tulbaghias are charming small plants (to sixteen inches), and they provide a mass of color with little effort on your part. Every window should have some.

Tulbaghias really grow quite well in a pot of rich soil. Set

SPREKELIA

rhizomes about one inch apart, ½ inch deep, in a shallow (eight-inch) dish. Plants usually bloom about six weeks after planting; then they will need good light and plenty of water.

You can choose from *T. fragrans* or *T. violacea;* the latter has a slight odor of garlic—and hence the horrible common name.

Tulipa (Tulip)

We are all familiar with the beauty of tulips outdoors, and there are so many kinds, it boggles the mind. Their beauty is well worth the effort indoors, where they add seasonal color and make a striking picture at windows.

You can buy potted tulips at your florist's (generally sold as gift plants), or if you are adventurous, try starting your own. The bulbs must have a period of coolness to bloom, and many people put them in the refrigerator for several weeks. I generally plant several bulbs in a six-inch pot and place them on a porch or in the garden, where temperatures are cold but never freezing. I move them indoors when buds have formed, but I do not try to carry them over. They really require outdoor conditions for another season of bloom.

Vallota (Scarborough Lily)

This South African evergreen bulb has dazzling red flowers on ten-inch stems and is a joy to see. Flowers generally appear in the spring or summer.

Set the bulbs with their tips protruding above the soil in the smallest pot possible (these plants like to be crowded). Give them a bright but not sunny place and water moderately. Repot only when pot bound. Do not be disappointed if the plants do not bloom the first year because vallotas take time. The main thing is to provide good drainage, so you might want to include, say, ½ inch of gravel at the bottom of the pot to ensure rapid

TULIP

drainage of excess water. Feed the plants every two weeks and keep them growing all year.

Vallota bulbs are expensive but worth it; the species you want is *V. speciosa.*

Veltheimia

These plants from the Cape of Good Hope bear pendant flowers red-tinged in a dense cluster head on a stout stem.

Start the bulbs in late fall, one to a pot, in loose soil. Be sure there is good drainage, and keep the soil fairly dry until growth starts. Then soak the soil thoroughly throughout the growing cycle. Feed the plants every two weeks and grow them cool (55F) but in full sun. Let them rest for two to three weeks in early fall to promote buds; after the plants flower, let them grow on until the leaves turn yellow. Then stop watering and store the bulbs in their pots in a cool, dry place for about two months. (Just keep soil barely moist.) Repot in fresh soil; veltheimia will produce a new harvest of flowers.

V. viridifolia is the popular species.

Zephyranthes (Rain Lily)

Don't let the botanical name put you off; these are beautiful flowering plants that do grow well with pot culture. The plants bloom in early spring, summer, or in fall on bare stems; grassy foliage comes later.

Plant four or five bulbs one inch deep in an eight-inch pot, using a rich soil. Water just enough to keep the soil moderately moist. Grow the plants in full sunlight except in summer, when some shade is necessary, and keep them cool at night (55F). When the pretty flowers fade, let the foliage mature fully, but in the fall give just enough water to keep the soil from caking.

Zephyranthes are generally sold in packages, in mixed colors rather than separately according to species. However, for those who want specific plants, Z. *candida* is white; Z. *grandiflora*, rose, and Z. *citrina*, yellow. These are truly delightful plants, so do give them a try.

List of Bulbs

Botanical and Common Name	Height, in Inches	Color	Bloom Season	Remarks
Achimenes (rainbow flower)	12	many colors	summer	good for baskets
Agapanthus (lily of the Nile)	16	blue, white	summer	fine color
Caladium	30	many colors	spring	foliage plants
Crinum 'Ellen Bousanquet'	30	wine red	summer	dramatic
C. *giganteum*	30	white	summer	huge flowers
C. *moorei*	30	white	summer	sweetly scented
Crocus zonatus	12	blue	fall	temporary plants
Cyclamen	20	pink, red	spring	good color
Eucharisgrandiflora (Amazon lily)	36	white	summer	amenable house plant
Eucomis punctata (pineapple lily)	20	white	summer	well-drained soil
E. *undulata*	20	green	spring	well-drained soil
Gloriosa rothschildiana (glory lily)	60	red, yellow	summer	dramatic

BOTANICAL AND COMMON NAME	HEIGHT, IN INCHES	COLOR	BLOOM SEASON	REMARKS
Haemanthus coccineus (blood lily)	30	scarlet	fall	never flood
H. katherinae	30	red	spring	stunning
H. multiflora	30	red	spring	never flood
Hyacinthus (hyacinth)	24	blue, white, pink	spring	great fragrance
Ixia maculata (African corn lily)	24	yellow	spring	easy plant
I. speciosa	16	white	spring	easy plant
Lachenalia tricolor (cape cowslip)	20	pink, orange	winter	small but lovely flowers
Lycoris aurea (spider lily)	36	orange	fall, winter	large flowers
Narcissus (paperwhites)	30	white	fall	a favorite
N. soleil d'or	30	golden yellow	spring	exceptional color
Ornithogalum arabicum (star-of-Bethlehem)	24	white with green	winter, spring	watch for aphids
O. aureum	24	yellow	winter, spring	watch for aphids
O. thyrsoides	24	white with brown center	winter, spring	watch for aphids
Oxalis bowieana	10–12	rose red	spring, summer	does well indoors
O. cernua	10–12	yellow	spring, summer	does well indoors

Botanical and Common Name	Height, in Inches	Color	Bloom Season	Remarks
O. hirta	10–12	rose pink	spring, summer	does well indoors
O. rubra	10–12	rose	spring, summer	does well indoors
Sprekelia formosissima (Jacobean lily)	18–24	red	summer	vivid color
Tulbaghia fragrans (society garlic)	18	lavender	spring	flowers one month after planting
T. violacea	18	lavender	spring	smells like garlic
Tulipa (tulip)	24	many colors	spring	good for one season
Vallota speciosa (Scarborough lily)	24	scarlet	summer	needs excellent drainage
Veltheimia viridifolia	20	yellow, red	spring	needs loose, fibrous soil
Zephyranthes grandiflora (rain lily)	16	rose, pink	summer	lovely indoors
Z. candida	16	white	summer	lovely indoors
Z. citrina	16	yellow	summer	lovely indoors

[CHAPTER 8]

꧁ ❀ ꧂

Vines

Vines are overlooked by home gardeners, and yet many of these climbers, such as bougainvillaea and morning glories, can beautify the indoors as they do the garden. Unfortunately, vines grow rapidly so they do require space. However, if you cut and prune, you can keep the following plants in bounds.

Bougainvillaea

In Florida this magnificent trailer decks outer walls with vibrant colors. Indoors the plants can decorate windows and other areas where drama is needed.

Bougainvillaeas are definitely not easy to grow, but they are not impossible. One of their idiosyncrasies—the main one—is location. Several times I moved a plant a few inches one way or another, and the results were amazing! Outdoors these brightly colored flowering plants like a lot of sun and heat, but indoors they seem to require coolness at night to be at their best. They need a well-drained, sandy soil and buckets of water, especially in the warm months, when they put on their show. In winter

Bougainvillaea never ceases to please with bright red flowers that can add a vivid color accent anywhere. (Photo by author.)

they can be cut back and kept cool and dry. Repot plants the following spring for another harvest of bloom. Give bougainvillaeas ample space to grow and large containers, say ten inches in diameter. In most cases you will have to supply some support such as a pot trellis, for the plants to grow on.

There are two varieties I have successfully cultivated indoors: 'San Diego Red' and 'Barbara Karst,' which is not as floriferous but is just as colorful.

Clematis

These beautiful outdoor vines with flat-faced, colorful flowers are universally admired.

The plants are fast-growing and require large tubs with rich soil; add a handful of limestone to the soil. Keep clematis in your sunniest window and train it on a trellis staked in the soil of the tub. Water thoroughly and frequently and use a liquid plant food at every second watering. These plants are available in season as prestarts, ready for planting, and I suggest you use these rather than try to start your own.

Clematis does not always adapt to indoor growing conditions; it seems to prefer an outdoor life. But what a joy it is to get it growing, and what satisfaction to get it to bloom! So when you feel adventurous, give this one a try. Most clematis in gardens are of the 'Jackmanii' varieties and will be designated this way when you buy them.

Convolvulus (Morning Glory)

This perennial climber has white or pink flowers, providing quite a bonus of color indoors in spring and summer. Convolvulus are not magnificent indoor/outdoor plants, but because they grow so easily, they are recommended.

CLEMATIS

Morning glories will always put on a bright, splendid show at windows. (Photo Burpee Seed Co.)

The plants require a soil heavy in humus. They need good sunlight through the winter but can be grown in a bright place the rest of the year. They grow vigorously, so a light rather than a heavy feeding every month is all that is required. Sow the seed in the same pot the plants are to grow in. A moderate temperature of 65F will suit them just fine.

C. cneorum is the species generally available.

Dipladenia (Mandevilla, Mexican Love Vine)

This South American vine bears magnificent large, funnel-shaped pink flowers throughout the summer and will grow indoors all year. The plant loves as much sun as possible and a sandy soil laced with charcoal. It requires abundant water, and

M.G.V. 75

DIPLADENIA

once dipladenia adjusts to its surroundings, it grows lavishly. Best in hanging baskets or on shelves, dipladenias are certainly worth space at home. The plants can be purchased, or you can start your own from seed.

Not readily available but worth the search are *D. amabilis* and and *D. splendens*.

Jasminum (Jasmine)

You can bring the fragrance of the outdoors indoors when you grow jasmine in pots. If kept in bounds, these vines are easily grown in small or large pots.

The plants need loose, fibrous soil and manure feeding every two weeks to encourage flowering. (Manure, almost odorless, comes in tidy packages and can be purchased at nurseries.) Because jasmine does grow well in shady places, it is ideal for indoors; only in winter will it need a sunny window. Jasmine needs temperatures from 50 to 60F. Do not repot more than once every two years; the plants seem to enjoy cramped quarters. Keep a vigil for aphids and red spider mites that occasionally attack jasmine. For a unique effect, put supports around window jambs, and let jasmine frame the window.

J. officinale, the most popular species for indoors, has white flowers. *J. nudiflorum*, with yellow blooms, is somewhat more difficult to grow indoors. Both are generally available.

Lathyrus (Sweet Pea)

Sweet peas at the window? Why not? These fine climbing vines so quickly cover a window with color that sometimes a jungle is the result. Their lovely oval leaves and generally rose-colored blooms appear freely in a sunny spot.

These plants need plenty of water and a good rich soil. They can be started indoors in fall for late winter bloom or in spring for summer bloom. Give the plants ample support and pick off seed pods to lengthen the blooming time.

L. latifolius is the most popular species, but many fine varieties have been developed.

Manettia (Candy-Corn Plant)

This old-fashioned vine is rarely grown, but it does have some qualities that make it a worthwhile addition indoors. It bears yellow-tipped red, tube-shaped flowers off and on throughout the year. Manettia is generally available in nurseries and is highly recommended because it grows with minimum care.

Grow the plants in warmth (75F) in a rich soil and in a bright location. Pinch back the new growth at tips occasionally to induce side branching.

Manettias can grow quite large, to four or five feet, so prune as needed to keep them in shape. At a window manettias are quite pretty all year; blooms pop out every few weeks in succession. Young plants are best so plan on annual replacement by rooting cuttings in the spring. *M. bicolor* is the most popular species.

Passiflora (Passionflower)

Years ago I grew these plants at the windows of my Chicago apartment, and their quick growth and mammoth flowers made me feel like an excellent gardener.

The plants require a lot of care and are only good for the season; but while they bloom they are well worth the effort. For any gardener with a passion for flowers, they present a worthwhile challenge. Passifloras need good, rich soil and buckets of water; it is incredible how much water they can consume, so be prepared to water and feed heavily all summer. Like bougainvillaeas, they need space and sun to do their best.

The two species I have always grown are *P. caerulea* and *P. trifasciata*. The plants have gained in popularity, and there are some improved varieties of *P. caerulea* at suppliers.

Plumbago (False Phlox)

This is actually a rambler, with blue, phloxlike flowers in loose clusters on the tips of new growth. A succession of blooms from early spring to summer makes it a worthwhile addition to the window garden.

Plants are available in one-gallon cans from suppliers. Or start seeds yourself. Give plumbago high humidity and bright light during the spring, summer, and fall but rest them almost dry in winter. Use a good, rich soil, with perfect drainage. Pinch back young plants to encourage robust growth. Mature plants, which can get leggy, also need pinching and trimming, about twice a year.

Plumbago is a handsome and desirable plant, but it does require a cool environment. Generally, night temperatures of 50 to 55F are necessary; during the day warmer temperatures are fine. The plants grow quickly and tend to become quite large, so be prepared—place them where there is ample space. Ask for *P. capensis* from suppliers.

Russelia (Coral Vine)

This wiry shrub has such a trailing habit that it is included in this vine section. The light green, feathery leaves and tiny, tubular red flowers make a pretty picture at the window. The plant may be difficult to find, so you might have to start your own from seed. Mature plants require a fibrous soil and partial shade, rather than full sun. Keep the soil quite moist and spray the plants with water frequently because they like a saturated atmosphere. A warm place, say, 70F, is best for the coral vine. Do not be afraid to trim and pinch as necessary to keep the plant within bounds.

I am particularly fond of the coral vine, and whenever I see one for sale, I buy it. Generally, I find it in a nursery that specializes in rock or alpine plants. The botanical name is *R. equisetiformis.*

Stephanotis (Madagascar Jasmine)

This is by no means an easy plant to grow—outdoors or indoors. But the effect is worth it. Stephanotis has lovely, glossy, dark green leaves and small, white star-shaped flowers that are incredibly perfumed.

This is a fast-growing climber and will thus need a trellis support, as well as space. The plants form buds at 6oF; if temperatures are any cooler, they do not bloom. Near-perfect drainage is essential for healthy plants, and a daily misting with tepid water helps considerably to promote good health. Feed stephanotis with a mild fertilizer every two weeks from spring to fall but not at all the rest of the year. Keep stephanotis shaded, especially in hot weather, or it soon wanes. Keep a plant in the same pot for two or three years; it objects to repotting and, indeed, may take some time to get settled and ready to bloom.

S. floribunda, the species generally sold, is available a few times a year at nurseries.

Thunbergia (Black-Eyed Susan)

This plant has defied me for years. Yet every year I try it again because of its magnificent orange flowers. Thunbergia grows quickly, does best in a sunny place, and requires lots of water during the warm months. Black-eyed Susans will bear their crop of flowers indoors if treated in this manner, but invariably my plants contact red spider mites and die in a few weeks, no matter what precautions I take. Perhaps my failures may be your successes—although I have not been in tune with thun-

The popular black-eyed Susan, with its profuse orange flowers, is a beautiful midsummer sight. (Photo courtesy George Ball Inc.)

bergia, you might be, so do try it because it is worthwhile. Make new plants every year from cuttings.

The species most sold is *T. alata;* recently there have been some improved varieties available.

List of Vines

Botanical and Common Name	Color	Bloom Season	Remarks
Bougainvillaea	red	late spring	always handsome
'Barbara Karst'	red	summer	good color
'San Diego'	red	summer	very colorful
Clematis 'jackmanii'	pink, blue	summer	difficult but worth a try
Convolvulus cneorum (morning glory)	white, pink, blue	spring, summer	good in baskets
Dipladenia splendens (Mexican love vine)	pink	summer	can be beautiful
Jasminum officinale	white	spring, summer	fragrant
J. nudiflorum	yellow	spring, summer	
Lathyrus latifolius (sweet pea)	pink	summer	fast-grower
Manettia bicolor (candy-corn plant)	red and yellow	summer, fall	not showy but easy
Passiflora caerulea (passionflower)	white and pink	spring	gigantic flowers
P. trifasciata	red	summer	stellar
Plumbago capensis (false phlox)	blue	spring, summer	nice, bushy habit
Russelia equisetiformis (coral vine)	coral	spring, summer, fall	blooms a long time
Stephanotis floribunda (Madagascar jasmine)	white	fall	difficult but worth a try
Thunbergia alata (black-eyed Susan)	orange	summer	floriferous

[CHAPTER 9]

⤳❧ ✿ ❧⤶

Trouble in the Garden

You probably will not be bothered with insects if you keep your indoor plants in good shape. The sick, weak plants are the ones that insects love, so watch your plants carefully. If you catch insects right away, the old-fashioned nonchemical remedies will eliminate them. If you have to resort to chemicals because of a heavy infestation, try some of the less noxious insecticides available.

Is It Insects?

Do not immediately assume your plants are crawling with insects if something is awry. Check to make sure cultural conditions are okay by first asking yourself the following questions:

1. Is there a draft on the plant?
2. Is there too much sun? Too much shade?
3. Are you watering the plant too much? Too little?
4. Is the plant getting too much heat?
5. Are you overfeeding the plant?

If you can answer No to all these questions, insects are probably at work.

Mealybugs have wreaked havoc on this plant; catch insects before they get a real foothold. (Photo by Matthew Barr.)

A closeup photo of mealybugs. (Photo courtesy USDA.)

Recognizing Insects and Pests

Now that you know for sure insects are at work, how do you identify them? First, inspect the leaves (tops and undersides), stem axils, and crowns of plants—the favorite hiding places of insects. Here is what the bugs and other pests look like—and what they do to plants.

Aphid. Aphids are black, red, green, or gray, oval-shaped, soft-bodied insects about 1/16 inch long. Aphids cause leaves to curl or pucker.

Scale. Scale are tiny, oval-shaped, and generally brown in color. They cause leaf as well as stem damage.

Mealybug. Mealybugs are soft, waxy, and oval-shaped. They cause a plant to wilt.

Red Spider Mite. Spiders are almost invisible but leave telltale webs. They cause leaves to look pale and stippled.

Thrips. These tiny, slender, winged insects leave a silver, sticky residue on leaves.

Slug, snail. Although slugs and snails are not technically insects, they are pests. Snails have a shell; slugs do not. Both creatures eat holes in leaves.

Eliminating Insects

Nonchemical Remedies

The following nonchemical remedies are not as thorough as chemicals, but they are safer and do not leave any noxious odors.

1. *Wipe and spray* with tepid water. Clean the leaves with a damp cloth and mist frequently. This will eliminate any insect eggs before they hatch.

2. *Use alcohol on cotton swabs.* Apply directly to mealybugs and aphids to effectively remove them.

3. *Use a toothpick.* Hand-pick visible insects.

Scale is evident on the stems of this plant; these hard-shelled insects require your immediate attention or they will destroy your plants. (Photo by Matthew Barr.)

4. *Wash away insects.* Use a strong water spray.

5. *Use cigarette tobacco* steeped in water for several days to apply on scale. (You will have to repeat applications several times.)

6. *Use soap.* A solution of ½ pound of laundry soap (not detergent) in two quarts of water will eliminate aphids and mealybugs. Spray or douse the mixture on the bugs; repeat applications every three to six days for three weeks.

Chemical Remedies

More than one dose of chemicals will be necessary to completely eliminate insects. Keep poisons on a high shelf or in a locked cabinet (and do *not* leave the key around!) so children and pets can't get at them. Malathion is the best all-purpose chemical because it does not have an accumulative effect; other chemicals are listed in the table on page 155. Take the following precautions with all poisons:

1. Chemicals will not work on a bone-dry plant; water and mist the plant first.

2. Never spray plants in direct sunlight.

3. Follow directions on the package *exactly*.

4. Stand at the proper distance indicated on the can when using sprays.

5. Make sure you have sufficient ventilation in the areas where you are using chemicals. The poisons can harm membranes, throat, and so forth if inhaled.

6. Douse insects if they are in sight. A whiff of a spray will not accomplish much.

List of Chemical Remedies

Name	Insects It Attacks	Remarks
Black Leaf 40	aphids, mealybugs	a tobacco extract, relatively toxic to children and pets but safe for plants
Diazinon Spectracide	aphids, mites, scale	good but more lethal than malathion
Isotox	most but not all insects	effective but toxic to children and pets
Malathion	aphids, mites, scale	broad-spectrum insecticide, fairly nontoxic to human beings and animals

NAME	INSECTS IT ATTACKS	REMARKS
Meta-Systox	most but not all insects	effective but toxic to children and pets
Pyrethrum	aphids, flies, household pests	generally safe
Rotenone	aphids, flies, household pests	often used in combination with Pyrethrum
Sevin	all insects	comes in powder or dust

NOTE: Aerosol bombs: generally sold under different trade names, these insecticides can harm leaves if sprayed too close; they can also irritate your lungs. Do *not* use any outdoor spray for indoor plants.

Index

[125]